I0437537

Saving the American Dream: The Path to Prosperity

A Blueprint of the 21st Century Economic Model

By Patrick Kelley

iUniverse, Inc.
New York   Bloomington

Saving the American Dream:
The Path to Prosperity

Copyright © 2009 by Patrick Kelley

All rights reserved. No part of this book may be used or reproduced by any means, graphic, electronic, or mechanical, including photocopying, recording, taping or by any information storage retrieval system without the written permission of the publisher except in the case of brief quotations embodied in critical articles and reviews.

iUniverse books may be ordered through booksellers or by contacting:

iUniverse
1663 Liberty Drive
Bloomington, IN 47403
www.iuniverse.com
1-800-Authors (1-800-288-4677)

Because of the dynamic nature of the Internet, any Web addresses or links contained in this book may have changed since publication and may no longer be valid. The views expressed in this work are solely those of the author and do not necessarily reflect the views of the publisher, and the publisher hereby disclaims any responsibility for them.

ISBN: 978-1-4401-3455-5 (pbk)
ISBN: 978-1-4401-3456-2 (ebk)

Printed in the United States of America

iUniverse rev. date: 4/28/2009
Cover Design © Jonathan Rios

For my Grandmother Louise Kelley
and good friend Curtis Pankow

Here are the means and ability to reconstitute the domestic housing market, create tax relief, universal health care coverage, and effectively increase individual wealth both domestically and internationally; achieving the reason for any economic system – the individual as the end purpose and the system as the means to that end. The legitimacy of government is in creating, maintaining and ensuring through political and legislative means this purpose – the individual as the exclusive end, to which economics is the basis for government.

Content

INTRODUCTION

1. HISTORICAL AND FUTURE MODEL FOR ECONOMIC STABILITY

The economics of a nation have the greatest influence on the direction and course that a nation will chart, in both the localized domestic policy and foreign relations/policy. Economic realities extend beyond ideological propositions that politicians far too often hold to while all reason, history and successive thought exposes fundamental flaws within the ideological basis itself. To achieve stability on both the domestic and the global stage a new visionary policy and fundamental change to the current economic model is necessary. To achieve long-term stability and growth a necessary evolution must occur within the economic structure and comprehensive model itself. The regular expected failures of the current system as seen in recessions are not a necessary component of an effective system, but are obligatory under a flawed system as currently in place. However, those with power do not easily change. The basis of that power is entrenched in finely honed old world systems that have long tradition and methods that benefit the smallest number of people. Regardless of the level or involvement of government or structure that it assumes there is one static principle, that a very small number will be the final decision makers and architects by which all levels of the social structure are determined and finally based. The question then is how much input and possibility does the individual within the structure have available to them then, and it is to this question that the economic model must be geared to answer. Creation of an environment where personal accomplishment and success are possible, where the sole basis is the individual's needs and where dreams are attainable, this is the fundamental design for which the system must strive - each person as the end goal not as the means to that system.

To achieve a systematic means that views the individual as the sole end requires the development of a new 21st century economic model. The development of this model must first begin to revitalize the domestic markets and basis of those markets, but then must go further, becoming the basis of a functional global market as well. The foundations of technology and the development of real-time communication are the basis of an effective and dynamic new economic model. The development of technology has fundamentally changed the manner in which not only nations but also the individual interact with their world. The business and economic interests of nations and individuals is no longer centered within artificially created arenas of commerce, that precluded the average person from becoming an effective player in the greater market either by the lack of personal experience or knowledge. The individual could once enter into the market place as player only to the degree which knowledge or experience allowed. Today, every individual is a more effective player regardless of the knowledge or experience that once was a prerequisite to meaningful participation, and it is technology and instantaneous communication that have opened the doors for true commerce and trade to the whole of society – domestically and internationally.

Technology and communication have also invalidated the premise that a nation is a stand-alone entity with minimal concern for global affairs and markets, which has been repeatedly shown throughout history to be flawed, but was sustainable due to the limited ability for interaction of nations in real-time conversation and the limitation of players in the market. Today, whether desired by the nations of the world or not, technology and real-time communication has created a neighborhood environment where the local corner store is only a click away. That store may geographically be located as far away as Bangladesh, but its impact and accessibility is no different from the corner store. The difficulty that is associated with the concept of a global market on the personal level is more due to generational difference, not due to usage or applicability. Successive generations have grown-up in a world where all the information that could be sought lie waiting at their fingertips with the click of a button. This accessibility and ease of use has fundamentally changed the manner in which people interact and in which the world will have to base its assumptions, governmental structures, economic models and educational systems.

Today's economic model, from the independent nation state to the international community, is premised on the limited interaction of each nation except at the highest level of government, and even with modification the basis of that interaction is fundamentally designed for long periods of silence in the process of information exchange. The modifications that were designed to accommodate a new world economy while maintaining an old world system meant for limited purpose have once more begun to crack and throw the entirety of the international community into fear and unsure waters. The historical perspective has taught the outcome of such dangerous waters where financial ruin become the norm and insecurity of livelihood and home weigh upon the minds of men and women. The current economic model, systems and institutions intended to stabilize individual nations and the international community are the root of the destabilization domestically and internationally. Due to flawed structure and limited functionality, the current economic model actually engenders a reality where the devastation of war and conflict would be a necessity to reinvigorate the systems and institutions within that model. War is the unfortunate and only result of such flawed models, systems and institutions, because war is the ultimate re-set button for the current economic model and thinking. War is a devastating answer with minimal benefit, but does produce short-term security of economy and nation, not in the sense of life but in a recreation of an archaic system.

The geopolitical landscape is ever evolving with ever-greater dangers and landmines waiting for the misstep of an unaware traveler. The traditionalist mindset is unable to make the next evolutionary leap in the development of global growth, and future growth is dependent upon the economics of each individual nation and the entirety of the international community's economics. The inability to think beyond the archaic economic model is willful ignorance or denial, rooted in adherence and blind devotion to traditionalist thought and institutional protectionism. The result of that blind devotion to political ideology and adherence to a flawed system that are in direct opposition to one another can be easily seen today, and the lesson(s) of history stand ready to teach their devastating truths once more. The basis of the fundamental change necessary must begin with the focal point of the archaic system. The United States must move forward into the future or allow itself and the world to become victims of the past.

The economic model that United States of America and the world currently operate within requires a reset when there is more than one globally effective economy. The system also has no room for the United States of America relinquishing its place as not only the primary economy but also as the facilitator of every other economic system internationally. The system as currently exists is premised on all manner of information, technology, production and miscellaneous services extending directly or indirectly through the United States at some level. The re-emergence of foreign economies and the development of new economies globally have unalterably changed the United States as the central point of all international trade and political currency, a change that the archaic model is not equipped to support. Minimal adjustments or minor modification(s) will not fundamentally affect the current economic model, systems and institutions nor resurrect or recreate the security that once superficially existed. The adherence to the old world system and mentality rather ensures, unfortunately, that conflict and devastation must forever remain part of the global psyche, and that it can only be through such devastation and conflict that the system can be salvaged or protected.

The benefit that is reached through conflict, such as during World War Two, is based on the individual players/nations that are able to minimize damage to their infrastructure, such as the United States. The United States through World War Two was the greatest beneficiary of the global conflict that ravaged our world. The United States was able solely through such global conflict and devastation to foreign economies globally to recreate its economy and pull itself out of a national depression that had no end in sight based on the limited social program policies of the Roosevelt Presidency and Congressional representation of that era. The harsh realities of the global conflict were born in flawed economic models of the previous era and the political pettiness that supported these segregated policies and models, both domestically and internationally.

The benefit to the United States by and through her involvement in World War Two was threefold. Firstly, the United States was able to salvage an economy and economic model that was then (as is today) unsound. The United States was then able to become a major global player and international voice, and lastly the United States was able to dictate the direction and means by which foreign nations developed their economies to adhere to the sole remaining functional economic system in existence – the U.S. economy. The United States had the luxury of an infrastructure that had not been destroyed let alone damaged during the course of the war, and because of this undamaged infrastructure was able to provide for all of the global community during the pre-war years (1932-1941) of the United States and then during and after the conclusion of the war. The entirety of the rebuilding efforts and monetary needs of the world were met by the United States, making friend and foe alike direct or indirect dependents of the United States. The American economic system was one of strength and ability but only so long as the rest of the world was dependent and non-competitive. That world no longer exists primarily due to U.S. policy and provision that helped reconstitute the international community's economic systems, and further helped to create an environment where newly emerging economies had the possibility of viability and stability - temporarily. However, the fundamentally flawed system mandated future economic difficulties and eventual collapse/implosion, in lieu of a great enough conflict that would again reset the archaic model to a superficially functional level.

The argument that war has no benefit to an economy is true longevity wise but not necessarily true in short-term resolution, correction or re-emergence. The venture of war is the most profitable means to creating an artificial economy with all the trappings of stability and liquidity. The U.S. entered World War Two during a massive depression at home and globally, and limited old world thinking ensured that the United States would be forced into the global war or face internal conflict. The entrance into the war achieved what no social engineered policy could ever achieve, the creation of a solid job base and the employment of a nation with a product that would be in demand with the prospect of new technological development possible through the military industrial complex. The secondary effect was the immediate involvement of the entire national psyche in one common goal, defeating an enemy that jeopardized America's way of life and basis of government.

The government began a massive employment campaign by and through the military branches of government, and industries came back to life and jobs were abundant and in need of workers. The induction of millions of Americans into the military brought about a job security for those inducted and allowed for less dependency on domestic production for personal use. The government became the largest employer of the nation and through this employment the men and women in government service were able to meet their needs (and wants) of food, clothing or housing – the three main concerns of every person. The private sector of industry was dependent upon the war effort as its basis of reconstitution and productive purpose – a world at war was profitable domestically. The benefit of such a large segment of the American population in government employment (especially military service) was that as cold as it may sound it meant a reduction in population; the dead have no need of a meal, clothing or home. The global population also benefited from the devastation for the same statistical truth that has no interest in human striving or concern. As tragic as any war is, as devastatingly destructive and insane in its very act, war nevertheless under current economic models and thought are an inevitability that must occur to reset a system that is incapable of providing anything more than short-term success and stability to the people which depend on an economy for a functional society at all levels.

Today, the same domestic and international economic crises are effecting our world, but to much greater extent due to technological development and much greater interdependence of the international community. The political pettiness and social programming (progressive liberalism) are pushing the United States and the world rapidly toward the edge of that abyss once more. Today, unlike the era of global devastation that allowed the United States to come to the forefront of global politics and economic basis, a resetting of the system will undoubtedly wreak such massive devastation that not even the United States will remain untouched domestically (infrastructure). The blind devotion to political ideology has become so detached from a living, breathing and reality based world that ultimate failure will be the result of the unthinking adherence and unwillingness to abandon untenable abstract idealism. The flesh and blood concrete reality of the world is the foundation from which the hope of the future is attainable. Through accepting the actuality of the world versus the idealism, the possibility of reaching the ideal becomes possible. The 21st century economic model is the basis of that concrete application.

The 21st century economic model must offer a means by which both short-term and long-term stability can be achieved, and long-term stability is only achievable when every person and nation has a vested interest in forsaking war as a means of economic return or basis of technological growth. That world does not currently exist, but with a willingness to move beyond traditionalist thought and protectionism that world is possible. It is only through the creation of the 21st century economy that the realization and aspirations of men and nations can hope to endure and find protection. The interest of the many will also become the vested interest(s) of the few that reside in halls of power in every nation and society of the world. An infinitesimally small segment of the world's population currently dictate the direction and basis of the overwhelming majority, and when this small segment is incapable of moving forward into the future then it is the vast majority that must pay the price and sacrifice to protect their archaic systems, institutions and limited thinking.

The future requires a more communal approach to business and economic growth, and this is not to mean a socially engineered policy or anti-capitalistic system. The system must be socially beneficial but conversely is one premised on the fundamentals of capitalism and free enterprise and the industry of the individual. A two-layered system that holds at the domestic/national level the traditionalist's economic model to a greater extent, and a dynamic global market place at the international level that views each independent nation as a business entity or household of individual standing. Already the world functions internationally on this principle but in a dysfunctional manner due to the segregationist policies of the old world political and economical mindsets. The interaction of business has gone beyond definitive national identification or ideation, today's global economy has created a new identity that is based solely on growth and potential that is not limited to specific nation states

– except the artificial limitations traditionally imposed which create a dysfunctional global market place.

The dysfunctional market will expand and then implode destroying the security and peace of individual nations and eventually the global community, as is being witnessed currently in the domestic and international markets based on the archaic economic model. Economic principles are philosophical in their abstract conception, but it is in the concrete application that the strength or weakness of such abstract thought must prove itself as applicable or merely idealistic. The ability to move beyond an abstraction is the most difficult of all endeavors for it requires more than mere theoretical and hypothetical espousing, but requires the vision to see the actuality of the abstraction in a real-time world where variables, intangibles and externalities are implicitly understood to exist and therefore not ignored or minimized for convenience's sake. Bringing the abstraction of many ideals into a functional concrete world and reality is the basis of and sole purpose of the 21st century economic model. The model must go beyond the immediate need of creating liquidity within the market place as desperately needed today. The model must lay the foundation of creating true liquidity that is self-sustaining, and ensure the prosperity and safety of the people. The application must affect the immediate needs and the future consideration of the individual's goals, aspirations and hopes as its truest test of viability and validation.

The basis of a 21st century economic model is one of innovation and potential, a potential that allows for the possibility of securing the ideals and dreams of all people. A global community does not entail sacrifice of independent national identity any more than the local community entails the loss of family or personal identity. The global community is moving beyond barriers and traditional structures designed to separate people, and because of technology creating the neighborhood environment on a global scale. Already the distance of people is no longer one of meaning with communication technology and the internet. The communication of people and nations goes to the very heart of creating a world in which peace is attainable, and the means of conversation are dictated by economics, whether they are functional or dysfunctional. The attainment of peace and moving away from the concept of conflict and war is unachievable through the premised idealistic ideological philosophies of a utopian world that does not exist. To achieve the possibility of that utopian world and ideal the realities and concrete nature of the world that does exist must first be accepted then addressed in appropriate and effective manner.

The traditionalist's archaic economic model and system(s) are what maintains the divisive and separatist nature that still exists today. The origination of that system was essential to the growth of the independent nation and international community at its inception, but its time has passed, and so now, the world must move forward into the future or perish in the past by reset through destructive means as tradition dictates.

2. THE UNITED STATES
A GLOBAL LEADER

The principles of freedom, liberty and the pursuit of happiness that have been secured in the United States can be secured globally through the example of America's bold action to reconstitute its own economy and develop the model by which the rest of the world can learn and adapt for the 21st century global economy. The United States faces many domestic challenges currently due to the flawed policies and inability of the traditionalist mindset, but these challenges are not so great as to be impossible to overcome. Current thought and the mentality of the old world political and economic schemas are frantically searching for some means to reconstitute their dysfunctional system. The ideological party divisions are further pushing America as well as the global community closer and closer to the abyss' edge, while pinning all of the world's future hope that by some magical means all will just get better. There is no future except for the direction that history has shown repeatedly, the commitment to war, death and destruction as the only viable means to resetting the archaic economic model. The real question is whether the world can survive another reset. Each generation and mass conflict of successive generations has become even more deadly costing ever-greater numbers of human lives, and catastrophic natural and social damage.

The future does not have to be one of limited possibility and unworkable abstractions found in socially engineered philosophies and political ideologies, but rather can be one of unlimited possibilities and workable concrete application through capitalistic principles that are based on a solid foundation that provide for the betterment of all people no matter their national identity. America once led the world into a new world of possibilities and political freedoms that extended from the people to the people, and so today it is America which must again lead to the new dynamic principles by which freedom, liberty and the pursuit of happiness may be secured.

The United States developed a political system and ideal that viewed freedom, liberty and the pursuit of happiness as the basis of its formation of government. The concept of a government of the people and by the people went against every traditionalist mindset regarding government. The sole basis of government is that it served the people, to be by and through the people themselves as the only legitimate means of government and governance. The United States came into existence at a time when every notion of government viewed the people as servants to its own end. By all standards of thought and history, any government that found existence and legitimacy to rule by the consent of the people was doomed to failure. The great minds that understood knew that this was not how governments were formed or run, if it were to last. The naysayer of that era and even today in some quarters argue that democracy and freedom cannot last because the people are incapable of ruling themselves, that the people are too unintelligent to determine the devices of their own future, which the people without massive government to dictate purpose and direction will fail and suffer inevitably. The argument is one of enslavement and weakness. The American psyche to a degree accepts this argument, as is seen in the ideas of altruism and that some external force is the cause for the individual's success or failure ultimately. The idea that governmental agents and politicians are better equipped to make life-altering decisions for the person is more than repugnant, it is an insidious enslavement of more than just the body but the mind and potential of the individual at all levels. An ideology that asks, no demands that each man, woman and child become a palm upturned beggar in wait of their portion, and that their portion should be secured and doled out by individuals that claim to know and understand better than the people themselves.

However, the people of America have proven the naysayer wrong at every turn in the face of adversity and snubbing of traditional governmental and political ideation. The American people have created an idea and form of government that allows every individual to achieve by and through their own hard work, dedication, discipline and commitment. The American idea of freedom is not one of social engineering and dictates, but is one of choice and sacrifice to achieve the individual success that creates the national success and strength. However, it is the traditionalist mindset and the fearful that have begun to undermine the paramount American virtue that never before took breath in the world, freedom of choice for individual success.

Once more, the United States must lead the world into the future by first reinvigorating its own economy, but must do so without jeopardizing the future of millions of Americans through wild spending sprees, massive bail-out and stimulus packages that could at best delay the inevitable by treating symptoms of the economic woes but not the fundamental causes. The means to correcting the woes of the United States are not extravagant nor do they require massive amounts of future tax burdens through the liberal idea of spending without limit or reason. The backbone of the American ideal and the ideal of every American is the ability to own home and property, and this ideal is under such strain it is nearing the breaking point.

The first step then to creating the new world global economic model is securing the domestic market within the United States, and this means recreating and stabilizing the mortgage industry and housing market. Correcting and retooling the housing market will be the basis by which all other aspects of creating a 21st century economic model will be possible and feasible. The process requires no further money creation or tax burden on the American people and begins to return financial security while creating true liquidity.

SECTION ONE: PROPERTY REVITALIZATION

Simplicity for Stabilization of Mortgage Crisis and Long-Term Growth

I. Initiating Recovery and Re-investment

The best means to salvage the mortgage industry is to allow the players with the necessary capital to acquire these notes and holdings of defunct lien-holders by and through auction. The government need only facilitate this process by stepping in (which has already been done), taking the holdings/notes into trust and then auctioning these holdings and notes. The companies and individuals that purchase these notes would then re-finance with the individuals in these homes to a truer market value.

Reinvestment and Stabilization through Auction

By use of an auction, the holdings of companies purchased would then allow for a transition of defunct institutions to more stable and capable companies and/or individuals. The price of the notes to auction should be set at a level that not only makes purchase very enticing but also allows for greater return on the investment. A price between 10-20 thousand dollars per note would not only allow for greater ability to purchase and transference of notes, but would also allow for greater security for individuals that have notes held by these defunct companies. The properties and holdings would no longer be in limbo allowing for the means to stabilizing the whole of the market by and through the individual and property itself.

An assessment of the community's market value would then dictate the re-negotiated note's ultimate value. Homes that had seen the market value artificially inflate to unconscionable levels would then be re-set to an appropriate value and a set interest rate for the home/property mortgage that then lessens the monthly payment to a likewise appropriate and manageable level.

A retroactive application of the homeowners' investment in accordance with the new monthly payment would begin to re-instill confidence in the market while also creating the much-needed liquidity in the general market. As example of this principle:

> A previous monthly payment of $1,200 a month which, by and through re-negotiated note lowers the mandatory minimum payment to $800 a month. The $400 difference would be applied to the length of current investment.

With (as examled) -36- months already invested the surplus $400 from each month would be applied to the current time investment. The difference of previous payment and newly calculated payment would equate to a one month payment for every two months already paid. An existing -36- month investment under this plan would give to the homeowner an additional -18- months worth of investment on the home/property. The previous -36- months would now become sum of -54- months in overall investment. The manageability of payment and worth of investiture would begin to stabilize the market while also re-invigorating the confidence of homeowners and buyers. The additional benefit is with the now freed up monies previously dedicated to mortgage payments would be able to be infused back into the economy in a myriad of individual ways creating the much needed liquidity.

The key to the success of this plan is the reinvestment and stabilization aspect, to insure homeowners do not suffer from what would otherwise be a devaluation of property. Each home within the market that is currently in jeopardy as well as those homes that are not yet in jeopardy by the collapsing of the market would gain benefit by and through this plan. There is an immediate impact of this plan for both actual reinvigoration of the market and the individuals within that market at all levels. There is also long-term benefit through this plan. Homeowners or prospective buyers are now more able to move into new homes of greater value or get into a first home. The money that exists within the economy already would begin to flow again benefiting both the lenders and borrowers, essentially bringing back the confidence necessary for liquidity and overall stabilization.

The creation of a separate entity to hold all of the money gained by and through the auction as well as the bailout/stimulus money already apportioned. The application of a high yield interest rate is necessary for this fund to ensure its viability for long-term use and existence. Portions of the money from this fund would be used during initial reinvestment and renegotiating processes for those homeowners that have fallen to far behind in payments as a means to bring their home/property back to even standing. The fund would be a long-term solution and separate entity from governmental apparatus that is designed specifically for crises pertaining to private properties effected by declared natural disaster situations. The fund would be available to the federal and state authorities when a determination of need is officially recognized. The receiving agents (federal/state) would then be under obligation of repayment at a low yield interest rate to ensure the fund's vitality. The individual states would be able to draw upon the fund that would connect all states and keep the fund viable. The surplus of this trust fund, placed into an interest bearing account would create a future source of liquidity for catastrophic circumstances (such as natural disaster or like occurrences) that insurance providers could apply if immediate funds are insufficient to meet promised policy coverage through the receiving state agency. The state would then have an obligation to the fund with any receiving insurance provider having obligation to the state for repayment of money's borrowed, for the purpose of declared emergency/emergencies. The means of acquiring disaster relief funds by state and local government, insurance providers and the individual(s) in need of the monies is then streamlined, while also bringing a greater connection and working relationship between the private insurance providers and the state and local government agencies.

Summary:

The effect of the above would accomplish bringing back both the free market system to this industry and alleviating the concerns of the homeowners. The re-established confidence would begin to ease the failing sense of security within the market and for the homeowners. The confidence renewed would halt the plummeting values and be the starting point of true and effective recovery. The eventual re-adjustment of the markets and the home values to a realistic level would begin the process of saving homes bordering on foreclosure (as well as to a greater extent rescuing homes that have already gone into foreclosure and bringing these homeowners back into their homes without default penalties), while also rewarding the financially disciplined. Paramount is the protection of the homeowner and economy, while also bringing stability to the market.

The money that would remain in trust beyond the initial re-investment back into the newly refinanced homes would allow bringing notes to par with time investment of the homeowner that is nearing retirement or fully realized. Protection for Americans' ability to own a home and retire is an essential aspect of this model. This "Rainy Day" fund would be nearly one trillion dollars drawing interest and have specific regulation and purpose, creating an independent insurer of the nation and individual states during time of crisis. The effect on free market insurance carriers would be positive, allowing for the stabilization of rates, rates determined by a myriad of created and natural events.

The primary benefit of this plan would mean no further taxpayer contribution, but rather the involvement of the companies and individuals that have proven themselves responsible and sound in the management of their own financial houses. A free market economy would respond to such action in the most positive of ways. The money that would be freed-up would create liquidity, a true liquidity based upon the money already within the market.

SECTION TWO:
Greater Wealth through Effective Federal Taxation Restructuring and Universal Health Care Based on Free market Principles and Capitalism

II. Restructuring Individual Taxation

To make an immediate impact on overly strained finances of average Americans, an immediate suspension of tax obligation for individuals earning less than fifty thousand dollars a year individually and for families earning one hundred thousands dollars or less combined. The numbers of individuals within these current tax ranges have minimal liability to none at all. Individuals and families would be better able to determine where their money is spent or saved based on their individual need. Instituting a transitional tax for those that would exceed either of the exemption status classes creates a safety net for individuals beginning to realize greater individual wealth. For an individual that makes $50,001 to $62,500 a year end tax liability of 10% and for those that earned $62,5001 to $75,000 a 20% liability. The application of the single income principle carries over to combined income earning families. A combined income of $100,001 to $125,000 would fall within the 10% liability status and the combined income of $125,001 to $150,000 would fall within the 20% liability status. After passing these limits traditional tax obligation would remain unaffected. The focus on these levels of income would reach the majority of Americans in a direct, immediate and meaningful way.

Summary:

The greatest benefit of this proactive approach is not only short-term benefit but also the long-term effects based on a solid foundation that will extend well beyond momentary difficulties to stabilize future aspirations. The secondary effect would be to allow a short-term influx of already existing capital for reinvestment by the individual into areas of his or her-own discretion over a longer period-of-time. The long-term effect would be more profound than a government generated stimulus check that would require future tax liability of the current generation and its successors. The stimulus checks and minor reduction in tax liability or creation of credits are far too limited and are reactive in nature. The reactive nature of these measures can only have minimal effect on short-term concerns while creating even greater difficulties long-range due to the nature of re-activism. A solid foundation for immediate, short-term, mid-range and long-term change are achievable if the policy and legislative changes are proactive.

The immediacy of this change is the most effective means to returning the confidence to the people that are suffering under the faltering economy and crisis, while also setting the means to achieving other stated goals of the government while maintaining the economic viability of the people. The purpose of taxation is to achieve societal needs of the individual within the collective social structure. When the people become impoverished or less able to meet the needs of their lives by or because of the tax levied then the tax should not exist. The taxation of the individual must never be detrimental to the individual or the society as a whole in its application. The principle of the individual tax obligation is to make the individual the end purpose, and that purpose is the betterment and possibility of elevating the personal living conditions of the individual by and through financial means, as well as protecting their lives through such means as affordable and adequate health care.

III. American Health Insurance

The ability for Americans to achieve a universal health care system is impossible under the current taxation system. The traditional thought or conventional wisdom argues that even greater tax burden is necessary to achieve centralized health care as seen in more socialistically based nations. These nations have historically developed differently than the United States and have traditions far different and diametrically opposed to the concept of a true free market economy where each individual is the sole determiner of his or her future, success and achievement. The idea of massive government that dictates the means to success of the individual is not an American tradition.

Centralized health care by governmental discretion and direction is ineffective within a free market system, and only offers minimal benefit (at best) while conversely impoverishing a nation due to such lethargic structure. Direct dictate by governmental agents or agencies is a socialist system that creates greater bureaucracy and less effective management. Every American that has ever dealt with any governmental agency when in need has met the convoluted lethargic and ineffective processes engendered by such direct governmental involvement and dictate. Americans need an effective means to achieving health care within a free market system that is dynamic, outside of federal government dictate and control, and goes to the heart of every American's ingrained belief in independence and self-determination.

Re-directing the previous Federal Tax liability toward health care benefits will lessen the burden of the individual in obtaining health care due to affordability issues. The redirection of money would insure that every working American, not just full-time employees, had access to health insurance. Already federal programs exist for unemployed Americans to obtain, or access, health care until they are able to secure gainful employment. The contributive factors of the working American helps not only provide a means to self-reliance but also rewards responsibility for the commitment to work at all levels and type of work. The prior federal liability would have either its entirety applied or a designated portion of the liability applied toward the employee contribution of provider cost.

STRUCTURE:

Validating the idea of using tax dollars as a means to securing that every American has access to health care is achievable by using the already existent tax system, with a redirection and usage of the money that is collected based on the principle of taxation. The retention of the basic principle of paycheck deductions remains, while effectively increasing the take home wages and providing the opportunity to have health care (which is unaffordable for a great many Americans). The conventional wisdom of creating a national health care system is fundamentally flawed and unworkable, partially due to the number of recipients that must be eligible, and partially due to the political structure necessary for such centralized health care. Nations of smaller populations, economies, job base and greater traditional governmental dictate have found success with nationally based health care, but these nations are almost exclusively dependent upon the government apparatus to provide at almost all levels of societal existence. However, the success of these centralized government run health systems are arguably less effective beyond general practitioner care.

The use of the current federal tax system principle is achievable while maintaining democratic principles of freedom and choice versus traditional socialistic principles of restriction and governmental control. The goal of universal health care is not only achievable, but functional and applicable under capitalistic principles that enrich the people versus socialistic policy that impoverishes the people. As an example of the principle, a pay-stub based on a forty-hour workweek, at fifteen dollars an hour with current deductions compared to the change with the removal of health care coverage liability (the previous federal liability now applied toward health care coverage – as is explained in detail in the following).

$15 Hourly pay rate at 40 hours a week	= $600.00
Deductions With Health Benefits	= $156.20
State Income Tax	= $19.86
Federal Income Tax	= $52.56
FICA/Employee	= $35.36
FICAMED/Employee	= $8.27
Dental Coverage	= $4.80
Medical Coverage	= $24.00
Voluntary Disability	= $8.33
Vision Insurance	= $0.94
Voluntary Life	= $2.08
Take Home After Current Deductions	= $443.80

-V-

$15 hourly pay rate at 40 hours a week	= $600.00
Deductions Without Health BenEFITS	= $116.05
State Income Tax	= $19.86
Federal Income Tax	= $52.56
FICA/Employee	= $35.36
FICAMED/Employee	= $8.27
Take Home Minus Coverage Deductions	= $483.95

From the example above the additional amount taken home by the individual at the end of the year is $2087.80. The "help" that the current administration and Congress are offering is essentially an additional $13 to $18 take-home per paycheck. The individual still pays all of the above (using the example) which works out to roughly $520 (at an additional $13 a week take home) to $936 (at an additional $18 a week take home) increase by end of year. The current governmental leadership also is adding a credit of $400 to $1000 depending on individual or combined income status. Should the government give every American within the range the $1000 credit plus an additional $18 per take-home check the increase for the individual works out to be $1,936.

A few other factors and numbers that need consideration using the current leadership's and congressional plan versus an American based system (using the above example). The final difference in yearly take home pay between the above example of an American based system $2087.80, and that of the current leadership's (Socialist based system) $1,936 means $151.80 less by year end with the leadership's idea of "help".

The second major consideration taken into account is the additional take home offered through the current leadership's plan based on the pay period. The basis of the above example given is on a weekly pay period, multiplied by the 52-week year. The leadership is making the statement that per paycheck the individual will add $18 (using the upper most number already floated by the leadership to argue for its plan) to the take home amount. Then for a bi-weekly pay period would mean an additional $18 for a total increase of $36 per pay period or (as seems to be the case) a total of up to $18 per pay-check regardless of weekly, bi-weekly or monthly pay period. The actuality is that it is up to a total of $18 per pay period, which then translates to halving the total yearly increase of the individual due to a 26-week multiplier of the $18 rather than a 52-week multiplier. Taking the additional $18 take home per bi-weekly check (pay period) comes out to a yearly increase of $468. Take the $468 and add the $1000 credit (end of year) for a total of $1,468 increase. The difference then (with bi- weekly) is $468 less annually which now puts the total gain by the current leadership's (Socialist based) plan well below the (American based) plan proposed by here by $619.80.

The difference between the two plans so far ranges from taking home less by the leadership's plan (Socialist based) of $151.80 to $619.80 (American based) so long as we base the leadership plan at the higher value of $18 per take home check. The difference and benefit becomes even less appealing (for the leadership's Socialist system) if the number used is less than the $18 per take home check. For a great majority of Americans the take home difference will be closer to the $13 per take home check. The difference at $13 per take home check works out to be the $520 per year (weekly) or $260 per year (bi-weekly pay period). The range then, for the leadership's (Socialist based) help, ranges from $260 to $936 (difference in take home increase depending upon weekly to bi-weekly pay period), with an additional $400 to $1000 at year (applied to tax return, next year) for a rough range of $660 to $1936 – all depending on pay period and other particulars of the leadership plan.

The (American based) plan offered here (using the $15 hour, weekly pay period as example) increases year-end wealth by $2087.80 (52-week multiplier). The weekly addition is $40.15 (doubled in a bi-weekly pay period to $80.30) which is $27.15 (compared to $13 increase by leadership proposal) to $22.15 (compared to $18 increase by leadership proposal) increase per pay take home check for the individual. In total the difference between the leadership's plan ranges from $13 ($0.32 hourly increase) to $18 ($0.45 hourly increase) per take home check (halved if biweekly) compared to this American based proposal that equals $40.15 ($1 an hourly increase) per take home check (doubled take home if bi-weekly).

The leadership's (plan/idea) sole benefit is income, which is also less money increase and designed for short-term duration in part. The increase in personal income is not the sole benefit in this American based plan. A viable and effective means to universal health care by and through this American based plan exist. The long-term benefit to every American is health care insurance (medical, dental, vision, disability, life) as offered through the employer. The means of increasing personal wealth in the immediate term for greatest impact and effect while also creating future sustainable wealth and providing a means to insurance based on legitimate taxation is now achievable. An effective means that is viable and sustainable for the United States that increases both personal wealth and provides health care insurance does not exist, as the leadership and traditionalist mindset (of Socialistic ideation) never considered any means that enriches the people while putting government back to its proper place (a means - not the end in itself).

The basis of other ideas (Socialistic systems) has been to create even greater tax burden on the individual and/or companies in order to provide for a centralized governmentally directed health care system as is seen in socialist based government run countries. The tax dollars that already exist once redirected (an American system based on the principles of capitalism) will begin to achieve the sole purpose of the system and legitimate purpose constitutional government, securing the possibilities of the citizens that are the basis of the government. The retention of a portion of the already obligatory federal tax dollar up to, but not to exceed, $120 would guarantee every working American is covered. To continuing using the example, at the $15 an hour wage on a forty hour week the individual would pay into the system $52.56 (scaling upward on a bi-weekly pay period). The money is already taken out of each check and therefore a new tax hardship is not incurred, as traditionalists (Socialistic systems) firmly believe to be necessary. The retention of money that would be spent on health care costs are now the individual's to spend, save or pay down other debt. The offered principle of taxation is now effective and legitimate, which achieves the purpose of any potential tax principle, viewing the individual as the sole basis of its creation and not the enrichment and expansion of government. An effective manner of taxation is engendered where the individual citizen and collection of individual citizens is the sole end, not the governmental apparatus as is currently seen.

The increase in wealth meets the Republican Party's argument for less taxes and smaller more effective government. The redirection of former tax dollars meets the Democratic Party's argument for enriching the majority of Americans while also creating a viable universal health care coverage system, with the greatest difference being the use of the existing tax principle (American based plan) versus the creation of more impoverishing taxation (Socialistic based plan/systemization and massive government). The question that would then remain for both Parties is whether the arguments/platforms of their respective Party are truly to these purposes (the betterment of the individual as the end purpose) or not.

The use of these prior tax dollars as now applied (under this American based proposal) meet the stated goals of the government, enriching the people while also providing a universal health care coverage. The deeper change to the basis of the tax system meets the espoused argument of ensuring that every legal citizen of the United States is covered while also making it possible for poverty level, low income, middle class individuals and families the ability to become upwardly mobile once more. The deeper realization by this change is that if it is the purpose of the Democratic Party to provide better means to financial security and universal health care then it is by capitalistic principle and not social program or socialistic based systems or ideology. The Republican Party then, as espoused, has its idea of smaller government realized while achieving the betterment of the individual and individual collective citizenry.

At the individual level, every American that takes any form of employment would benefit regardless of full-time or part-time status. The coverage would begin immediately upon employment based on coverage plans already offered by the employer. The traditional waiting period of 90-days would no longer be necessary. The concept of COBRA coverage when leaving a job or out of work would remain in effect and the ability to take current coverage to a new employer would remain in effect. The primary benefit is the inclusion of every working American in a health care system that is universally applicable while also adhering to the free market-principles of capitalism and competition.

The competition of providers would begin to reduce the overall cost associated with coverage as greater numbers of Americans become involved in the system. The increase in coverage would also begin to create a need for an expansion in the health related fields in general. Capitalistic principle and free market systems dictate that as greater numbers become involved in a system or a product becomes widely used the cost associated with the system or product decreases, while competition within the providers of the system or product attempt to attract more customers through decreasing cost. The increase in the case of health care would be comprehensive coverage packages at a decreased cost to the individual consumer due to the number of consumers now involved. The other-side of this increase in consumption (and decrease in cost) is the need for a widening job base and ability to provide. The direct and indirect benefits of this change are exponential that involve not only the individual benefit as the sole purpose, but has the collateral effect of benefiting the entirety of the nation from health coverage to job creation and economic stimulation.

The most fundamental difference between the part-time and full-time employee would be the actual take home pay. The full-time employee would now keep the currently spent coverage cost taken from every check increasing the net-wealth of the individual and family unit. The part-time employee would see no difference in the take home pay as the previous federal liability (conceptually) did not end only shift its purpose and usage, but would now have the benefit of health care coverage. The increase in jobs and ripple effect would begin to let the entirety of the market begin to stabilize and correct itself, creating an environment where hiring, retention, training and building once more are reinvigorated.

The affect to the business community would be wholly positive which directly and indirectly effects the private individual, and so a more effective system is then possible to begin to achieve the interconnection of employer and employee in this system with the federal government's role only as facilitator (as was designed by the founding fathers and constitution).

Summary:

The basis by which this concrete application is achievable meets the ideological adherence of both major political parties, the basis by which taxation is justifiable, and viewing the individual as the end purpose exclusively. A redirection of already existent federal liability (tax) would bring the idea of a universal health care coverage out of the abstract idealism and ideas that currently exist into a concrete reality. The reduction to the federal government income would be minimal and at most would force the government to become more responsible in spending as well as more involved in oversight of programs for their effectiveness and contributive value.

IV. Capital Gains Tax Relief

The removal/suspension of the Capital Gains Tax is necessary to help create confidence in the markets and begin to bring back some semblance of stability in the markets and the business entities. Already, in the sphere of public and governmental conversation the pros and cons are under consideration for any potential change to the current system. However, one of the most important considerations with Capital Gains Tax is the effect on publicly traded companies and the stock market.

There is a great deal of consternation over individuals making obscene profits off of the stock market, it is those very same individuals and profits that are the driving force to the existence of market potential both domestically and internationally. The taxation was geared toward ensuring that the individual and/or company that saw profit through such sales and means of enrichment would not become corrosive or detrimental to the market as a whole, while also attempting to create some stability within the markets to minimize excessive sell offs for strictly short-term profit. The basis did have the intended effect initially and superficially does so today. However, an environment now exists where destabilization of companies is the norm due to profit margin concerns, concerns centered on a stagnant capital that is taxable while not being offset during times of inflation or other external concerns. The greatest protection for money is to achieve the highest return and minimize tax obligation is a continual acquisition and selling of stock, which in turn affects the finances of the publicly traded company or companies, and so the markets and companies are at the mercy of the capricious taxation on Capital Gains.

At a deeper level, the model created and accepted has the unspoken demand of continued and unhindered growth by any publicly traded company. A failure to achieve that level of growth endangers an otherwise stable company of being sold off creating and artificial downturn which (as seen in the market today in numerous cases) becomes a legitimate crisis that may lead to a financial collapse of the effected company and subsequent employees and related systems and structures. A failure of one institution is by no means an isolated instance that has no effect outside of the failing institution. The indirect effect on related fields and companies is the most damaging, due to the seemingly unrelated and independent nature for the cause of corporate failure. The Capital Gains Tax affects more than simply business and the extremely wealthy, the tax also affects the elderly and those that have worked for a lifetime and now depend on stock options and other related capital interest based money to support themselves in the twilight of their lives. Retirement is fast becoming an unattainable hope for a great many Americans due to the prohibitive taxation born in traditionalist mindset and flawed unworkable ideological adherence (Socialistic systems and basis).

V. Corporate Taxation Restructuring

Reducing the tax liability of corporations by 25% would allow for a more effective use of current capital to stabilize the companies themselves, while also securing health care affordability for employees at the employer level. The reduction and redirection of the previous tax then follows much the same principle as the personal income tax obligation change (American based as previously discussed). The difference would be percentage based versus a hard number cap used with the individual tax relief (eligible under the American based proposal).

The 25% reduction allows for restructuring, using half of the retained money by the company in a traditional manner, with the other half of the retained 25% applied toward the company's health care obligation. The money previously directed toward health care provision by the company would become free (liquid) capital for the company allowing for direct application or payment toward expansion or worker related benefits (i.e., pay, retention, hiring, etc.)

The principle of governmental facilitation makes for a more upwardly mobile individual bringing government once more to its appropriate place - the means. The redirection has an immediate impact while also laying the foundation for long-term growth and stability that benefits the individual directly/indirectly by the application to the corporate community. The means to health care is provided (at no further cost) to the individual or job providing community of the corporate world. The greater retention of earned money by the company allows for a sturdier foundation, which in turn amounts to greater stability for the employee and potential for increased wage or upward movement in general.

Corporations are based on profit margins and the greater the margin the greater the increase in employment and average earning of those employed. The company that is in the position to lay off thousands of employees is also the very same company that is employing thousands of employees, and the only means by which it is possible to employ thousands is increasing company profit margins. The basis of the profit margin are many but one in which the government can directly help facilitate to better this margin (and so indirectly by direct means increase potential employment levels and wage scales) is tax restructuring. The idea is not to make corporations tax exempt. The business community facilitates the existence of democratic government by its revenue, through capitalism and free market economics.

A truer statement of effective and realistic capitalism is when government is in its proper role of facilitator for the end goal of the individual, and the company is acting in its proper role of the means to betterment. Socialist based systems see business and corporations as an abuse from which the government must protect the individual, and subsequently must grow to massive controlling and dictatorial power to ensure this protection, but in doing so places the government as the end goal and both the individual and business community as a means to its own end. Purely capitalistic and socialistic systems are abstractions that are impractical and dangerously destructive to the individual and collective society of individuals. The most effective means to protecting the individual interest is in asserting the individual as the sole purpose of legitimate government, and so limiting government to the role of facilitator in domestic affairs by the means of the business/corporate community.

The possibility of achieving greater individual wealth and universal health care exist because of the wealth created by capitalistic principles, and so the ideal of achieving both of these stated goals is not through impoverishing taxation (Socialistic ideology/progressive liberalism) but rather effective taxation and greater free market reinvestment principles. Decreasing tax burden and shrinking of federal government creates a more effective government, as areas of constant involvement by federal government become more limited and specific to its proper place and role as facilitator. In time, the re-structuring of the tax system will create less need for federal government involvement at the individual level through programs and dictate, allowing the states and local government to be the better judge of their own communities' needs.

VI. Small Business Taxation Restructuring

The small business is an area that is at the heart of any restructuring of the tax system, and so revitalization is necessary to make the creation of the small business more realistic in their existence and ability to compete within such a diverse market place. The reduction of taxable income from the small business is essential in allowing these businesses and owners to have hopes of viability.

Restructuring the tax code in like manner for the mid-range income business as with the corporate restructuring will provide the same benefits for business operations.

The greatest difference in the restructuring of the taxation basis for the small to low range income business would be setting exemption from federal taxation up to a set earning level (and then using a transitional tax principle as previously discussed – American based plan). Removing the federal tax obligation for business that gross up to $200,000 annually would provide a means to stabilization for these businesses while also allowing for retention of capital that would better prepare such businesses for transitioning into mid-range earnings or the corporate setting. However, using the previous tax system (in principle) a means to withholding from these same businesses 5-10% of the previous obligation that would then be used toward securing health care benefits for employees would mean that no matter the size of the business health care would be provided. The provision of health care makes it viable for the potential employee to accept a small business' offered position, while making it possible for the small business itself to attract a wider pool of potential employees.

The premised changes are purely capitalistic principles that achieve the means to security of the business and individual and provide for a diverse landscape of financial opportunities for both the individual and business to secure their respective needs and wants. Once again, the benefits of health care provision are possible financially by the federal tax change and reaffirmation of capitalistic principle as the means to insuring the individual is the end purpose exclusively.

VII. Self-Employed Taxation Restructuring

The individual that takes the risks and challenges of self-employment should be one of the areas of protection. A good number are individuals that work within the agricultural community, but are not limited to these individuals. The local handy man to the struggling author and artist are among those that have taken all of the risks of financial ruin to achieve their dreams through self-reliance, and they should be within a system that aids them like every other citizen. To use the concept of the small business tax restructuring the self-employed tax restructuring is achievable in like manner. The greatest difference would be for greater federal governmental facilitation to ensure that these individuals have the means and access to the health care that every other member of the community has based on the taxation changes.

The means of governmental facilitation is not in governmentally run health care provision, but rather in collecting existing providers for competitive bidding to include this pioneering group. A 5-10% of total income directed to the health care providers would replace the previous tax obligation, achieving both goals of individual health care and personal increase in wealth. The means would ensure that these individuals have the same benefits and choice that the traditionally employed individual has, while also meaning a greater retention of individual wealth making them more upwardly mobile and financially secure.

The agriculturally based individual would now be in a position to begin paying down debt incurred under the previously impoverishing taxation system and scheme. The long-term benefit would be individuals that would be able to provide for their own retirement, be out from underneath growing debt and make the transition to higher levels of income at their own choosing or remain at a level in which they are comfortable.

Summary

The means provided are the blueprint and framework by which achieving individual security and universal health care are attainable. The immediate benefits are dramatic and begin a solid foundation on the path to prosperity while also securing a future means to maintaining a system that holds each individual as the sole and exclusive end of its very existence.

SECTION THREE:
Re-Vitalization of the Dollar and American Automotive Industry

VIII. Minimum Wage Reduction

A very drastic step in revitalizing the American economy is the reduction in the current national minimum wage level. Over the past seven years, an 85% increase in the minimum wage has occurred by some estimates. Minimum wage is the basis of the dollar's value (in part), as this translates into the amount of actual money in the overall economy, the more abundance of actual potential currency the less value that each dollar then has. The need to re-invigorate the dollar is imperative for a restructuring of the economic house.

The basis of the minimum wage is one where the employee's earning potential is unproven or has a history of incompetence, inability or instability and therefore is either an unknown financial risk to the employer or a known liability to the employer. The minimum wage also is the basis by which Unions and other employers base their expectations during negotiations and final pay offerings to new employees.

The reduction of an immediate 25-30% would create an overnight valuation in not only the American dollar, but also increase the wealth of individuals earning close to minimum wage – effectively benefiting the poorest Americans, primarily. The decrease in minimum wage would not mean a reduction in pay for currently employed individuals or pay scales or for those individuals with a firm offer of employment at a set pay rate (excluding very specific contracts that provide a specific pay rate at a set percentage above the established federal minimum wage).

Summary:

The greatest benefit to an immediate reduction would be the natural increase in the dollar's value. The buying power of the dollar would begin to reassert itself not only here in the United States but also in foreign countries increasing international trade rates while injecting more return value back into the United States for foreign investments and related industry.

The positive effect on domestic affairs would be companies holding off in layoffs or other cut backs to get through the difficult economic times, and quite potentially creating an environment where hiring and retaining of current employees is preferable. The retention or hiring of individuals would mean curbing the climbing unemployment rates and giving individuals the opportunity to begin to reassert themselves in the markets and personal finances. The argument that such a move would be corrosive to the common worker is ineffective and wholly untrue. As current levels of unemployment begin to rise it is effectively stating that no financial possibilities are being offered to the common worker, where as a reduction that insures job retention and possible employment meets the need of the worker – financial security or the possibility of such.

IX. Automotive Industry Re-Tooling

Currently the trend is to throw money at the failing automotive industries in the hopes that this influx of taxpayer money will help get through temporary difficulties and allow these companies to restructure in a meaningful way as to become financially viable once more. The difficulty with this is the belief (in the face of the reality) that there is only need of a temporary solution to the current difficulties and failures within the automotive industry. A fundamental change must occur to revitalize the automotive industry. However, the current and traditional mindset of minimal modification to an existent system dooms any long-term change while also being incapable of assuring even short-term benefit.

The means by which correction and intervention is being handled was designed for, and comes from, a system that presupposes minimal damage and only a short-term need of immediate capital while forces within the market correct themselves to more appropriate levels of manufacturing and competition. Today this mindset is further pushing the automotive industry toward the abyss' edge. A combination of old tools and new thinking is necessary for the correction and savior of this American industry, that, should it collapse would bring unprecedented calamity to an already crippled economy.

The first necessary action would be freezing price levels of new vehicles at the levels for the 2007/08 fiscal year. The next action would be a mandatory renegotiation of current Union contracts, bringing such contracts in line with other industrial wages and benefits. Issuance by all automotive makers that have received bailout money of vouchers for potential new car buyers during the fiscal year of 2009, these vouchers applied to dealership purchases and passed-on to the consumer by decrease in sticker price at the market level. The re-organization of the automotive industry is essential to solidify American automotive industries both domestically and internationally.

Summary:

The freezing of price levels at the known values of the 2008 fiscal year would allow greater affordability for potential car buyers in purchasing a new vehicle, while also having a static point, which engenders the feasibility of lending and vouchers. The secondary effect would allow for lending agencies to be better able to work out credit lines and free up money currently frozen due to such severe economic concerns as are faced today.

The designed voucher program is to reduce the cost of purchase at the dealership level, passing on to the consumer the savings. The reduction in cost would be another means to freeing up lending and extending credit, while also making it feasible for the potential car buyer to enter into the market once more. The influx of money would have the effect of creating liquidity within the market itself. The lower the initial cost of the vehicle the greater potential for a lending institution to be able to justify a loan, while also benefiting the consumer with potentially lower payments of shorter duration.

The reduction in contractual obligation that are currently in place would in part be addressed by the reduction in the minimum wage, as the minimum wage is the basis of the higher pay-scale for the automotive workers and unions in general. The reduction would also begin to bring profitability margins back within reach of the manufacturers. The collateral and peripheral industries would then find some measure of security in the knowledge that the industry itself is beginning to become viable once more, which could allow reasonable business owners to push through lean and difficult times.

The merger of the industry leaders is essential if the American automotive industry is to be competitive in the modern global economy that now exists. Traditional mindset and business models are outdated and will only hinder and eventually reach (if not having already done so) failure in a market where domestic competition is no longer the primary basis, as was the case historically. The need of the American business model to enter into the 21st century is imperative if America is to be economically viable, not only in the automotive industry but in every aspect. The automotive industry that is in such desperate need allows for this change which has industry benefit, and this change will also be a template by which future economic principles can be based for other American industries that are structured in similar fashion.

SECTION FOUR
Domestic Foundation for 21st Century Global Economy

X. Re-Tooling Monopoly /Antitrust Laws

The purpose and historical design of both monopoly and anti-trust legislation was to protect the American consumer and disadvantaged business from their very inception. However, the original protections that these laws were intended to ensure have inversely come to harm both American consumer and business alike. The detriment is not one due to flawed origination of policy and legislation, but rather by and through the evolution of segregated national economies as primaries to a global economy with an international primary basis.

A limited pool of domestic competition was the basis of these laws and policies. The era when such policy was sound does not exist today, and has not for decades. The American system lasted into the 21st century due primarily to a devastated world (economically) after World War Two. The United States was the sole beneficiary of the world needs' coupled with no external competition to meet those needs. However, with the re-emergence of defunct economies internationally and the development of new economic competition the limited and now fatal policies are exposed.

The government must revise and remove prior legislation/policies that are truly designed for domestic economic viability to create a more functional and dynamic international economic viability. The primary focus should be on commerce of significant value to international trade. A directed process of re-organization of major holdings (consolidation) is essential to America's future growth and viability. A strategic and methodological approach will be required to ensure the smooth and effective transition from the current archaic model to a more dynamic and robust 21st century model.

Summary:

The main benefit of re-tooling these companies and their holdings is the creation of a more competitive environment, both domestically and internationally. The monopoly and anti-trust legislation and policies once reworked will make the American economy stronger and viable in direct competition with other markets on the international stage. With the advent of new technology and the ability for instantaneous communication and information retrieval at all levels of society the previous ideology of localized competition and protections is no longer functional. The reality of the 21st century is a global community with a technology savvy consumer that relies less on the local market(s). The growth of the internet and ability to find any amount of product or service has created a competition unlike that ever known in the history of civilization, a market that through the immediate ability to connect to every potential vendor of service or product creates in and of itself competition and stability. The reality that exists in the world today is that any consumer in any part of the United States has access to internet use, and through this use access to a potential endless listing of available product or service sought. The ability to secure such product or service at a rate or price that falls within the individual consumer's price range. The effect of such is the market having created internally the safeguards of competition that the laws/policies regarding monopoly and anti-trust were designed to facilitate.

The current state of the American economic system (laws designed for primarily domestic based competition) has the adverse effect of making American business non-competitive at home and abroad because the competition is no longer a localized center as has traditionally been the case. The concern of American business leaving American shores for more business friendly environments is one of growing concern, and one that has and will continue to harm the domestic American economy as a whole (with an unwillingness to affect true change). The total wealth produced is slowly moving to foreign economies that by mere newness or developmental aspects have allowed for the growth of business and hence created a stabilizing effect on these foreign economies and their communities. The re-tooling of the monopoly and anti-trust legislation and policies will begin to bring American companies home, which will have the effect of creating future jobs and securing current jobs within the domestically based American businesses and economy. To keep the predominant amount of wealth produced by American based companies/industry will stimulate the domestic job sector, and produce long-term viability and stability domestically and internationally.

SECTION FIVE:
21st Century Layered Economy

XI. Differentiation of National and
International Based Interest Rates

The creation of an effective and dynamic global economy is essential. The 21st Century model requires a separation of domestically based economic interest rates that are limited to the function of the individual nation's per capita wealth distribution, and the global community's expansive and ever changing basis of wealth and distribution. The separation of interest rate principle for domestic and international value allows for greater leeway in direct action of the global community in stabilizing developing nations' economies, while also allowing the domestically based economies to become more solidly built and functional.

The interdependent nature of the global economy has in effect created a unified economy that is partially recognized with modifications of economic principles geared toward facilitating, but due to the fluid nature of global economics and flawed principles (political/ ideological considerations as basis), an ineffective and dysfunctional system is in place. Communication and interaction of nation states has become instantaneous. A real-time environment dictates real-time fluidity in the market place that is not dependent upon the inner working mechanisms of any one particular nation. The internal mechanism that were designed for the benefit of a particular nation's people, now hinders the ability for necessary change(s) of an immediacy that is today required. The current economic models cannot provide for the dynamic fluid real-time changes that are essential for a functional global economy.

The separation of domestic and international rate basis allows for stabilization of the domestic market place with an interest rate applicable to the needs and realities of the internal market focus of the individual nation. Domestic economics requires a more static principle due to a more static basis of wealth creation and distribution itself. The rate that applies to the primarily domestic economy is then more functionally capable of meeting the affairs of the nation, which stabilizes its potential interaction on the global level. Catastrophic events within the individual nation state have minimal global effect while allowing more effective domestic handling of the crisis. The development of unified global economy with each nation, in essence, being its own corporate entity (as effectively is the case today) is now more capable of assisting the effected nation by whatever means most appropriate (just as one national economy is more effective in dealing with a problem within the whole).

Traditional theory and the premise of isolated interaction of markets at specific levels of government and relegated to a small collection of companies no longer applies. The market place has expanded to include every nation as if each nation were a single state within one national identity. The policies and instruments designed for highly separate and independent national interests are now detrimental to the entirety of the global community because of their limiting nature. The current model is a closed model. A continuous re-thinking and modification of the current model for inclusion of new players and the exiting of traditional players creates a need for even greater modification, which has the adverse effect of more reactionary modifications in an attempt to accommodate the exponential growth of the global community both economically and population wise. The reactionary nature of such policy change engenders a short-term solution without long-term correction, and due to the separate nature of the current system, any fundamentally necessary changes do not occur due to an illusion of non-applicability to all nations. The time variable also has a dramatic effect on the global markets, which in turn reaches down into the individual nation states. The effect of bad policy and lethargic movement of a dysfunctional and archaic economic model and system come to fruition with the instability of governments around the globe, which in turn raises geopolitical concerns as to the ultimate effect of such instability.

Re-structuring the global economic model to be a true global economy that is inclusive rather than exclusive will have the effect of investing each nation individually in the welfare of the entire global community in more than an ideological or abstract concept of betterment/interconnection. To make such a change demands embracing the only system that can sustain the growth necessary for higher standardization of living and stabilization of such a diverse population – capitalism.

XII. International Basis

The primary basis of the global economy is credit and the concept of value of a designated currency, while the exchange of an actual currency is very rare. The purpose of business and economies at the stratosphere are dependent upon a valuation system that ensures that the specified value of the goods or services rendered is in line with other competing entities. Recessive and depressive conditions that have historically existed as currently exist today create the devaluation which then extends downward having far-reaching effect. The need of a system of valuation that is not dependent on any specific nation is essential to securing future global economic goals, which in turn will strengthen the individual national economies within the global market. The development of a unified currency based primarily upon the World Bank and collective value of the international community is essential. The development of a unified currency focused on a set value attached to the concept of the global economy as the basis of a credit system that would stand separate from the national standard, would then ensure valuation and allow for a more dynamic business environment that (through its creation) has the safeguards necessary for the global economy. Already the framework that could support such a system is in place, and the implementation of specific policies and re-direction of vital institutions would make such transition possible within a reasonable and protective manner.

The concept of a purely credit based global economic model allows for more fluidity in dealing with unexpected or dramatic changes, and also protects the entirety of the global community from the instability of any national standard monetary basis. The built in protection ensures a more stable market where valuation does not continually fluctuate based on the domestic concerns of any particular nation. The stabilization of the global market is a vested interest of every nation. The unified economic basis of the international community ensures that greater conversation begins to occur between nations when disagreements develop, and a more committed approach to resolving each individual nation's difficulties becomes an indirect goal of the collective family of nations.

A centralized credit basis allows each nation to incur debt and make payments more effectively based on the current and forecasted value of the market, much as credit ratings are already determined. The system is in place but it is not formally recognized (creating the dysfunctional system as is currently seen), and so all transactions are multi-layered to include the basic credit rating of the nations involved and then processed through various monetary systems creating more cost and dilution of the actual value. The current model also creates a barrier to emerging nations and economies from becoming fully invested and thus stabilizing their own domestic economies and political structures, while further distancing and bringing to an almost tyrannical dominance a very few economies. The subsequent difference in domestic policies then begin to further erode at the entirety of the market as smaller economic nations are incapable of competing globally, and enticing more aggressive actions of more militarized nations against more economically based nations that are not as muscular or capable of national defense due to domestic (population) realities.

The inclusion of every member at a functional level begins to negate the imagined gains of military conquest or armed conflict as a means to "level" the playing field, and brings less dynamic/robust economies to a somewhat even standing with the more dynamic and influential economies of the world. The secondary benefit is that the individual identity of the varied nation states are in no way transformed, allowing the political structures within these nations to remain intact at the domestic level which will only have a reflection on the potential credit rating of the nation. The means of this system would allow the capitalistic principle to offer greater hope to every nation while also allowing for the retention of more socialistic based governmental apparatus, until the nation is pre-pared, and capable, of making the transition into a more solidly based political and economic structure. Aspects of Socialistic principles are sustainable within capital-ism, whereas Capitalistic principles cannot exist within socialism, as Capitalism enriches and Socialism impov-erishes as the means to equality. The natural transition would bring the nation to a more dynamically robust and economically competitive level in time. However, no external forced change would occur to any nation's political structure to mirror that of any other nation, but would rather be able to make the modifications to their own independent governmental apparatus that is most effective to stabilizing their domestic economies based on their individual needs and current state of affairs. The global market that would include them would stabilize the national identity within the international community. In time, the functionally interrelated economy would engender greater political dialogue based in conversation rather than physical intervention or provocative rhetoric that divides.

XIII. Domestic Basis

The creation of a domestically based interest rate that has only application to the internal mechanisms and market place of the nation is a necessity in the creation of a layered economic system designed for the 21st century. An interest rate is the basis of the wealth and interaction within the domestic market much as with the global market, but with the fundamental difference of domestically limited resource and area(s) of wealth creation. The limiting factor of the national/domestic economy creates the need for an actual currency basis for the economic system itself, and the basis of the currency valuation is the interest rate principle.

The domestic currency is the greatest concept of wealth and wealth attainment by the majority of people, as the conceptual principle of wealth is only an abstraction used in a concrete manner. The international economics basis is conceptual with credit universally accepted as the coin of trade and wealth basis, but the domestic concern involves far smaller amounts of money that must be rooted in a firm physical realization – such as the dollar or similar identifiable concrete bridge between the conceptual abstraction of economics and wealth. The similarities of the international basis of economics and that of the national domestic economics are many, but the differences are profound. The international market and economy has an infinite potential in wealth creation, as the geographical limitations of national boundaries are not applicable in the course of trade. The domestic economy is, however, limited in its wealth potential due to the limitations of national boundaries, and the finite capacity of geography and political determinants.

Domestic economies are even more susceptible to failure or downturns due to their limiting nature, and the political considerations that they must address as well. The greater potential for internal domestic failure or downturn requires greater safeguard of the system, which not only produces the potentiality for wealth but also must maintain a stable currency that acts as the intermediary between the predominant population and business of the domestic basis. The basis of the domestic system is localized commerce, and the vast majority within the local system will be incapable of accepting any system that has divorced itself from a stagnant currency that has very little use except within the general community. Domestically based economies have and will continue to rely on nationally standardized currency, both as an identification of individual nationality and as a function of domestically based policy and governmental concerns.

Maintaining a national based interest rate is essential in determining the value of the currency that is in place. However, a differentiation of application of the interest rate to the differing aspects of internal trade and wealth creation is essential. The traditional application of one set rate that applies equally to both positive wealth creation and negative wealth creation is outdated and potentially lethal when modified in an attempt to redirect or correct internal crisis of the domestic economic system. A means of differentiation is necessary to begin to create a stabilization point within the domestic economic system. The differentiation of the positive and negative wealth creation allows greater flexibility in adjustment of percentage rate fluctuation, change either originating from the general economic community, or directed by the facilitation of the federal government.

The positive aspect of wealth creation is funds or capital/interest bearing accounts that take static investment for the creation of greater levels of wealth later. Individual Retirement Annuities (IRAs) is just one example of a positive wealth creation. The specific purpose for this wealth is the eventual goal of retirement or reduction in work investment by the individual and/or family unit. The current system endangers these investments (and other positively based wealth creators) by a reduction of the national interest rate designed to facilitate the negative wealth creation (loans). The loss of individual positive wealth places even greater numbers in jeopardy of being unable to retire. For those no longer associated directly with the workforce are placed in greater jeopardy of being unable to sustain their static living conditions, living conditions that were designed around an assumption of positive wealth creation.

The negative aspect of wealth creation is monies created through loans and other expenditures of capital on an investment that has a greater potentiality of devaluation due to purchase (such as a loan for the purchase of a new vehicle). The rate that effects negative wealth creation is quite often the rate that is most susceptible to change or becoming vulnerable to domestic economic climate change, necessitating its directed change by federal means. The desired effect of any change to the rate basis which is intended for making greater negative wealth creation possible has the unintended effect of lessening the positive wealth creation, and this cumulative effect creates the deflationary, inflationary and/or hyperinflation that can be so devastating to any domestic economy.

A separation of positive and negative interest rates will have the effect of allowing for action that is more dynamic without creating unnecessary negative effects in the entirety of the market in combating adverse economic conditions. The intent of dropping the interest rate was to free credit up (negative wealth creation) but had the adverse effect of degrading the positive wealth creation aspect of the economic system. The separation of the two areas of wealth creation is in effect a safeguard that creates a viable means to renewing and/or re-vitalizing the domestic economy, without the adverse effect of drawing even greater numbers of individuals and institutions downward by static universal interest rate policy application.

The focus of the domestic economy is to have in place safeguards that allow tools to be used that help an adversely affected area while not degrading other areas in the process. The evolution of the economic model is the creation of more effective and dynamically fluid systems and structure that allows for the greatest protection of the individual, nation and global community. The separation of the two primary areas for wealth creation and means by which they interact with both by the market and the direct action of government creates a stabilization of the entirety of the market for future growth.

XIV. Layered Structure Summary

The creation of a layered economic system would have shared principles but would also have safeguards by its very design, while allowing for the creation of small businesses (domestically) at a competitive level from their inception. A reorganization of standardization and rule sets is fundamental to such divergence. This separation will also help better protect the localized business during times of instability within the global community, having a good deal of separation from the major players in the global market. This separation will allow for the smaller business to remain viable during potential downturns or hiccups within the global market by being more resilient and not facing competition with the larger players with the capital to extend through (or create) such adverse economic climate.

The progression from securing the mortgage industry to the creation of a layered economic model is essential for the future global economy, which has developed. The traditional thought that one national economy is viable and dynamic enough to compete in the new global economic realities is an attempt to hold onto a defunct system. The growth of technology and communication have so radically diversified the players and changed the rules of the game, the manner of conducting business have been fundamentally altered. To hold to an archaic 19th century economic model will not only stifle but also decimate any potential future economic growth. The principles outlined go against traditional conception of economic models only in the sense that the new direction is one of fluidity and departure from stagnant inflexible rule sets that have undermined the security of individual nations and the global community.

The creation of a layered economic model is necessary for the United States and the global community as a whole to enter into the future with the hope of any stability in the face of the new economic realities. The traditional basis of the economic system has held as principle one singular system designed to facilitate all levels of economic interaction, whether between the local business, individual and/or the international community. Today, with the ability for instantaneous connection a separation must exist between the major corporations and governmental based entities of the world community, and the domestic based lower tier small business oriented entities.

The current conditions in the United States and globally are demonstrating the flawed and dysfunctional economic model's truth in the harshest of manners. This real world demonstration is not some hypothetical consideration nor is it limited to a specific industry or localized to miscellaneous communities, but is wide spread and has comprehensive ramifications that transcend the local economies, which are most visible. The ability to make these necessary changes lays before "we the people," with an entire world and nation looking to the United States once more for the leadership into the new world, a world that demands a more fluid and dynamic application of ideas and ability.

Following the formula outlined previously, the means to creating the layered system is achievable. The basis of this new economic model is making all of the necessary changes to the entirety of the system at the levels outlined above as well as other not already discussed areas of the current economic system (which will only become viable with the implementation of the fundamental changes outlined).

The creation of this two-layered economic system has the effect of including the protections and stabilization of international/global market place while also protecting the domestically based economies of the world. The ability to create and become viable as a new business owner is also not only protected, but is made even more possible which in time creates a much more diverse and competitive global market place.

The Congressional leadership as well as the Executive branch of government must work together to create the necessary policies and legislation that would be the foundation for the economic model. The primary necessity and obligation of making such a differentiation of economic models within one nation would be a separation and differentiation in which capital is gained and the manner in which wealth is measured (i.e., the form of currency which the related businesses use as a form of conversation and interaction).

The current model dictates creating greater potential failure in the overall domestic market because no separation exists with the interest rate, thus dragging down otherwise viable areas of wealth creation. The degradation of this portion of the wealth creation has made recovery through traditional means even more unlikely, if not impossible. A creation of massive debt by the government by using taxation further exacerbates the faltering economy both short-term and long-term due to limited money that must strategically be placed (both in location and time) with only the hope that such investment will have the intended effect of re-vitalizing the economy as a whole. However, due to no separation between the rates affecting negative and positive wealth creation the influx of money only repays a minor portion of already lost wealth while further devaluating the existing currency by the creation of new currency.

Current Thought and Discussion

The direction that the current leadership in the government wishes to take is one of short-term success (at best) at the price of long-term stability and growth. The reduction of the interest rate was designed to stimulate spending and free up money for loans, but none of the minds that argued for its reduction made mention of the growing population (particularly the elderly) that is dependent upon returns off of investments as the basis for their income or ability to retire. This older segment of our population is apparently, in the minds of the traditionalist and governmental officials, an acceptable sacrifice to help the physically, mentally and medically able (most often) individuals to have the opportunity to purchase vehicles and homes at lower interest rates. The unspoken decision by any individual or agency that accepts this policy is that those that have worked and contributed through the course of their lives are unimportant. To enjoy what are the twilight and golden years of their lives is unimportant. They should silently suffer and be abandoned for the sake of a system that is broken and flawed. The system is most important regardless of the insidious betrayal of the hardworking American by and through such policy/policies. The acceptance of this idea/policy is to support the idea that is (perhaps) fatally detrimental to the oldest segment of our population, and this is arguably the direction of the current policies and leadership – if not intentionally so then a truly frightening disconnect underlies the decision making process.

The major idea of the current administration is the creation of 2-3 million new (federal) jobs (over the next decade) for rebuilding our infrastructure. It is without question that we as a nation need to begin to tend to our infrastructure in updates, repairs and new construction. However, the manner in which the administration has chosen to pursue this goal is the shortsighted problem. The federal government should be facilitating private industry in creating jobs instead of creating even greater tax burden while shrinking the private job sector. The burden that will then be placed upon the working Americans at all levels to pay for these newly created federal jobs in both direct pay and subsequent benefit packages will have the adverse effect of driving low income families closer to the poverty line and a general shift downwards of the accumulative wealth of the nation as a whole.

The newly touted economics (Obamanomics) takes the idea of trickle-up compared to (Reaganomics) the trickle-down model. The concept for Obamanomics is that from the base of the mountain the river will flow up to the peak. Nature is effective in its design, and so we take our laws of physics based on the natural design. The natural design of nature is that the river flow from the small peak to the massive base that must support the entirety of the mountain itself. To force the river up the mountain (trickle-up economics) will mean massive governmental intervention, and this intervention requires the direct and/or indirect seizure of personal and national wealth. The seized wealth must then be under absolute control of government direction to determine where and how this seized wealth is used. This massive Re-distribution of wealth engenders absolute government control and dictate, effectively making the government the end purpose and the people subjects to government.

There is merit in minor aspects of each plan or idea offered by the leadership, but the negatives and detrimental realities of these plans so far outweigh the benefits as to solidly entrench each into a toxic stew that should not be digested, and if digested in their unmitigated offering will poison the host which feeds us one and all. The means to prosperity is through the people, and the self-desire of the people is the driving force. The parent seeks to have a better neighborhood because of and for his/her child, the selfish desire to protect that child. The selfish desire of the parent is the benefit of an improved neighborhood for the betterment of her/his child, but as the neighborhood improves, the benefit extends far beyond the parent and child. Today, we the people must strive for that selfish love that protects our children, and that same selfish love that extends outward to benefit and improve our entire world. True improvement comes from realizing the betterment of our own lives first, and it is through the self-desire of and for that improvement that dedication and commitment are born. This abstract altruistic idea of, "someone else first regardless of personal pain, loss or suffering" is the surest means to degradation and destruction, as in its very application it dictates that someone else — anyone else — is more deserving and in need and must come before you. The past has shown the pain and devastation through adherence to purely idealistic philosophies and political ideation. The mentality of the past is the surest way to achieve the results of the past.

To quote a man noted for his genius. "You can't solve a problem with the same mind that created it." Albert Einstein.

www.ingramcontent.com/pod-product-compliance
Lightning Source LLC
Chambersburg PA
CBHW031325290526
45784CB00014B/2146